Partners in Rhyme

Partners in Rhyme
Volume I

A Collection of Poems and Shared Words
By Sharon Johnson & Ryan Baird

This book is licensed for your personal enjoyment only.
Copyright © 2017 Ryan Baird & Sharon Johnson
All rights reserved.

Dedication

Sharon

Firstly, I'd like to thank God in Heaven for gifting me with the ability to write.

Secondly, I'd like to thank my Partner in Rhyme and good friend, Ryan Baird, for choosing me to collaborate on the beautiful book of poetry we've written together.

Thirdly, I'd like to thank all those friends who've always stood by me whether they liked poetry or not. They've never wavered in their support and encouragement.

And last but definitely not least, I'd like to thank all those people along the way, who may not have known me well, but saw my passion and given me many reasons to smile on those days I really needed it.

Ryan

To the many and varied friendships in my life, past, present and future. Without these relationships and experiences I wouldn't be half the man I am today. It goes without saying that I owe an old friend from my distant past. He showed me how to expressively vent during angry and often confusing times of my youth. Tim, thank you.

Preface

Sharon

I remember the day I first met Ryan Baird. It was Memorial Day 2015. I'd written poetry all my life, but had only started sharing it publicly for about 5 months. At the time, I wasn't considered a serious poet yet. Ryan asked me if I'd be interested in helping him with some poetry. I thought he wanted suggestions about how his poems might look on certain pictures or the kind of font he should use. I had no idea this would develop into us writing a poetry book together. Until Ryan suggested it, I'd never given collaborating with anyone a thought. I agreed and we began to work on our book. Ryan was like the hurricane you never see coming, until it's upon you. He walked into my life like a whirl wind. I'd never met anyone so excited about poetry ever. He climbed mountains even though he was scared of heights. He fiercely loves his family and was always a man of his word. He was as blue collar as you could get and yet, he was a true wordsmith and his words are some of the most exquisitely beautiful I've ever read. The poetry held within these pages are very different than most poems you'll ever read. We worked on our poetry with a particular theme from his view point and mine. We collaborated on several of the poems. We wrote in various styles such as; Rhyming, Haiku, Acrostic and Free verse. And he was gracious enough to try his hand at the new style of poetry I now love to write. Ryan and I have not only found a unique balance in our different writing styles: but over the past 23 months since we've created this beautiful book, we've became loving, caring friends with a connection and bond that will stay with us forever.

Preface

Ryan

I had reached a point in my writing that I felt I could confront the fear of sharing my words. Out of all the writers and poets I read on social media there was one fledgling poet and gifted writer that shone brightly. Mustering my confidence I reached out to who at the time I knew to be Sharon Johnson and now know to be my friend. She was incredibly gracious with her time and advice. During the development of our friendship we wrote, exchanged notes, shared stories and somewhere along the way we connected in a shared love of literacy. Not only could I share my poetry with Sharon I found myself being able to trust her with a collaboration. I had never considered this as an option but that it felt so natural was equally surprising. We challenged each other to write better, reach deeper and take this chance on one another. Sharon has now developed a style of writing unique to her during our poetic sparring. The results of which are crafted within our book.

Contents

Shared Words

Solitary Memories—Ryan/Sharon 17
Coarse Passing—Sharon/Ryan 19
Eventful Hope—Sharon/Ryan 21
Ambitious Unmasking—Ryan/Sharon 23
Remembered—Sharon/Ryan 25
Melodies Binding—Ryan/Sharon 27

Love & Faith

Loves Embrace—Sharon 31
Loves Embrace—Ryan 33
Easy Connections—Sharon 35
Easy Connections—Ryan 37
Heavenly Prayers—Sharon 39
Heavenly Prayers—Ryan 41
Joy—Sharon 43
Joy—Ryan 45
Hope's Gift—Sharon 47
Hope's Gift—Ryan 49

Erotica

Tender Aftercare—Sharon 53
Tender Aftercare—Ryan..55
Blissful Submission—Sharon...57
Blissful Submission—Ryan 59
Natural Affection—Sharon 61
Natural Affection—Ryan 63

Anger

Domestically Violent—Sharon 67
Domestically Violent—Ryan 69
Confined Silence—Sharon 71
Confined Silence—Ryan 73

Depression & Loss

Dreamscape Windows—Sharon 77
Dreamscape Windows—Ryan...79
Continental Drift—Sharon 81
Continental Drift—Ryan 83
Blue Rain—Sharon 85
Blue Rain—Ryan...87
Moments in Exile—Sharon...89
Moments in Exile—Ryan 91
Focus—Sharon 93
Focus—Ryan..95
In the Shadows—Sharon...97
In the Shadows—Ryan 99

Karmic Connection—Sharon 101
Karmic Connection—Ryan 103
Conversation—Sharon 105
Haunted Love—Ryan 107

Earthly Future

Planetary Dreaming—Sharon 111
Planetary Dreaming—Ryan 113
Worldly Tears—Sharon 115
Worldly Tears—Ryan 117

About the Authors

Sharon Johnson 121
Ryan Baird 123

Shared Words

Solitary Memories

Ryan/Sharon

Silence has greeted this man during solitary night's musing
Once again grieving alone, the heartbreaking memories abusing
Leaving these sad thoughts is something he cannot abide
In this sacred place he no longer has to act, no longer has to hide
Trembling with fear of a life spent without his lover's touch
Aching and empty without her, to feel anything is just too much
Resilience ebbing as he drifts through consistent hollow days
Years marching on by relentlessly, he can't move past this malaise

Missing days with this man that were filled with love
Every day they were together she thanked God above
Many times they made love all night, right through until dawn
Only their love made sense, constant and cruelly withdrawn
Right from the start he was the only man needed in her life
In a world full of lustful fakes he chose her as his wife
Experiences were a thrill and always exciting
Some loves are lost and all just as frightening….

Coarse Passing

Sharon/Ryan

*M*y life started out blissfully free from all worry and woe
I was closer to God, in his grace I believe and I know
*S*pirituality and faith found was always my saving grace
*P*lans, as I aged, very different as life changed pace
*L*ove always betraying me leaving me forever scarred
*A*ging older than my years, my heart has become hard
*C*ynical and unhappy, I watch my drifting life slip away
*E*ternity and close humanity is no longer child's play
*D*eath find me soon at your feet, I'm ready to kneel

*M*ortality the coil I know will not release or to heal
*O*f this life I chose to fight, to constantly want more
*R*ighteous as my surging anger is to this spirit I abhor
*T*o give up is not in my nature, to surrender is simply wrong
*A*gainst this eternal night denied, I refuse this swan song
*L*agging light will be a constant opposite to something so unholy
*I*ntimate is my knowledge of spectral death's touch choking slowly
*T*ime has slipped withering, a cold shock searching and clasping
*Y*earning secretly for the peace that oblivion will be forever lasting….

Eventful Hope

Sharon/Ryan

Years ago a woman of faith until life knocked her down
This distant memory vividly elusive and making her frown
Men came and went with them all her lost dreams too
Events made her fragile as cracks started showing through
Little by little pieces of her soul began slipping away
Hope once so precious diminishing day by day
Still there's a flicker somewhere deep within her soul
Faith that was missing, faith that would make her whole
Then one day fate intervened sent with a tender heart
Her hope restored never again will it depart…

Ambitious Unmasking

Ryan/Sharon

This mask an illusion, hiding true ambitions
Never hidden this life isn't what I'd envisioned
An often jaded past, a wished for radiant future
Will I be accepted or suffer more torture
A chance taken on a decision to change
I've no choice anymore, I have to be brave
This new strength forged in the crucible of lost glee
An impossible dream but it's my destiny you see
The vision of which has seen me soar into the unknown
So close now less afraid to unmask and start to be shown
How I have longed to be free from this mediocrity
Finally my coming out party because here I am, it's me….

Remembered

Sharon/Ryan

*L*ost in the memory that has burnt out her faith
*O*nce so strong and present before finding hollow hope
*S*oaring through the dark maelstrom of tortured emptiness
*T*he dark solitude of shadow's pain, biting and raw

*D*reams that were hoped for, now lost with familiar regularity
*R*emembered fragments of what was once so radiant
*E*choing memories of a shadowed lover and her elusive surrender
*A*ching with sharp loss and tightly held pain
*M*easured minutes tick on by and relentlessly march on
*S*lipping away to the oblivion of indifference….

Melodies Binding

Ryan/Sharon

*T*he pages of this melody were never meant to be found
*I*magination off key, this wailing dirge of forgotten despair
*M*eted out in switching tunes so distantly remembered
*E*mpty cloistered secrets, angelic in their holy acceptance
*L*ikened as they are to a haunting prayer from on high
*E*erie musings grasp desperately to divine inspiration
*S*aving the final release for symphonic variable movements
*S*tructured as the melodic harmonies are around this fallen faith

*H*appiness and joy are found in sweet laughter of younger years
*A*lways hopeful as we are to our imagination's conjuring of dreams
*R*estless energy fills our soul as we raise our hands to the sky
*M*emories stored of youthful pursuits bringing a smile to our face
*O*ur blissful songs sung as we dance freely in the pouring rain
*N*o limitations holding us back only those we put upon ourselves
*Y*es these are the things we remember as we enter our final dance....

Love & Faith

Loves Embrace

Sharon

Warm and tender
Passions ignite giving you
My total…
~Surrender~

You're my heart's aching…
Deepest Desire
Through your exquisite eyes…
~I see myself~

Your sweet words
Fill a void in a place…
Only you could ever fill…
~That space~

Making love with our lips…
Their touch on mine
Unsaid words…
Only loving sounds heard

The exquisite music…
Of two heart beats
In perfect rhythm
The dance of two souls…

Love's sweet embrace
~Becoming one~

Loves Embrace

Ryan

In this moment
In this time
We have discovered
~Our freedom~

Safe and secure
A private sanctuary
Secretly we jealously guard
~Our heart~

Tenderly we touch
Connecting once more
A tactile arousal
~Our passion~

Memory's knowledge maintained
Perceived by loving eyes
Embraced in hushed sighs
~Our history~

In this life
Or the next
I will know
~Our love ~

Easy Connections

Sharon

The easy connection I felt with you from day one
Was something unexpected and we'd only begun
You were like a cool breeze on a hot summer day
Was time to live out your dream, so much to say
Words we share have brought such joy to my life
With you, so easy and carefree no worries or strife
Such a short time together but we've both grown
An amazing friend one of the best I've ever known…

Easy Connections

Ryan

In sunrises glow has found my arms tightly embracing
This strong touch will have your heart racing
In a cherished whisper I say "It's you I adore"
Sighing softly, this happiness you can't ignore
How simple is this moment, kept structured in time
I have wanted this, needed this, in my rare downtime
Leaning into me there's no rush to start the day
Maintaining this intimacy we both want to stay
Reality pressing on our lover's composed requiem
No longer seeking freedom as it has already come….

Heavenly Prayers

Sharon

Lord in Heaven I
Pray for your peace that passes
All understanding

Lord God this is my
Humble and fervent prayer guide
Me through the darkness

I'm not sure what I
Need but I know you're the one
Who can grant me peace

Heavenly Prayers

Ryan

Prayer without sin
A gift from on sacred high
Selfless freedom sought

Coming to this place
A sanctuary of sorts
Blissfully alone

On my knees I pray
A higher power unknown
Confusing faith sought

Joy

Sharon

*H*ope springs eternal or so they say
*A*lways the dreamer come what may
*P*assion is what I live for every day
*P*erhaps I'm foolish to think this way
I am a dreamer my writing on display
*N*ow is my joy and my time to play
*E*very time I write I feel like I can fly
*S*ouring upwards touching the sky
*S*o I dream it doesn't matter why….

Joy

Ryan

Hilarity has come and it's here to stay
Azure skies found radiant, this wonderful day
Peaceful dreams finally found from on high
Pain however close fading by the bye
In this wondrous moment, such perfect timing
No need for worry, or any future pining
Escaping from my reality I rise, far away drifting
Slowly ascending, unrestrained as my joy is lifting
Suffice to say this rapture I'm happy to find gifting….

Hope's Gift

Sharon

As a young child, I was innocent still pristine and unjaded
I was brave, fearless and my life was easy and uncomplicated

When I got older and I started to see a different side of life
My optimism began to wane and my existence was one of strife

Every now and again the sun would peek through the clouds
That's when I'd raise my hands to Heaven and shouted aloud

I would often wonder did God hear my needy, aching prayer
Did he ever hear me, he was always quiet, and did he even care

It continued until that spring day I heard his rumbling voice
I could hear his soothing words of comfort telling me I had a choice

Something inside changed as the darkness lifted in my heart
That was the day that I happily decided I needed a fresh start

Since then my life is changed and my soul has been set free
Where once I lived in darkness, no longer blind and I can see....

Hope's Gift

Ryan

There are days I feel isolated in known company
The constant chatter, I find a tiresome symphony
I still don't know if there's protection in isolation
A self-made creation, my own private bastion
It's been said that I have been known to shine
Pulling away from you, no longer do we align
This shadow I have cast is dark and unsettling
Somehow through this, you stand before me trembling
A bright gift given for one who has lost his way
Gives rise to a brighter future and hope for another day
How could I fathom a life without you shining bright?
For when I'm wrapped in darkness it's you who brings me light
A proud man seeking atonement on his knees praying
Searching for your forgiveness, any price is worth paying....

Erotica

Tender Aftercare

Sharon

The relationship between a Dom and his sub isn't like any other you'll find
Many misunderstand the great care he takes of her body and of her mind
His sub willingly gives herself to him freely for his use for pleasure and pain
The Dom never forgets she holds all the power which he cherishes everyday
Today his kitten has done well and he smiles as he unties her hands and feet
He pulls her to him sweetly kissing her lips softly while he tends to her needs
She rests her weary body against him enjoying the feel of his tender touch
The one she always craves after their playtime and always needs so much
It's in these special moments their bond is renewed and trust reinforced
They've formed a unique relationship one of balance and a daily choice….

Tender Aftercare

Ryan

We have travelled to pleasures brutal heights
Raw and unfiltered we live for these nights
From a position of unspoken trust, to have you kneeling
This is my need, my desire, everything that I am feeling
Intense pain received and inflicted, my pride you have claimed
Abandoning all protection, you submit to being tamed
To give you the gift of restraint is something that I share
Shattering you into pieces, I will hold you till you repair
Physically exhausted, bruised, battered and meek
Sheltered in my strong arms your body feels so weak
Protected, sheltered and calming to a mind constantly awhirl
I have known you as my cherished whore, my one and only good girl…..

Blissful Submission

Sharon

I give myself willingly
Trusting you with all that I am
Knowing you'll always take care of me
Never pushing me too far
I may be your submissive but
Never below you only beside you
As we grow in our common goal
My need to please you is immense
I choose to serve you in every
Way that you ask
Your respect and admiration for me
Grows with each passing day

You've never looked past me
With eyes wide open you see me as I am
You've earned my heart body mind and soul
You've molded me like raw clay
Making me perfect in your wise eyes

When I was new and unsure
Your patience was constant
Willing to wait for your diamond in the rough
To become your un-cocooned butterfly
Beautifully formed into what you'd always known
You'd own me completely; you'd be my happy home ….

Blissful Submission

Ryan

To take what is willingly given
Ownership in guided trust and patient care
Trust an enveloping cocoon of hard desire
Restrained strength pushing against hard limits
Communication felt as you attend to my bodies' cues
Knowing what will please me pleasing you
Exposed as you are to my oppressive need
Fractured wants captured in close attendance
Molding carefully forbidden carnal appetites
As what is readily given is ruthlessly taken
Structured boundaries knowingly stretched
Every scene played out to proud eyes
To see you rise to tasks with wanton eagerness
Each painful reminder on skin's bruising memory
Wordlessly approval is granted by raging eyes
Your beast has become uncaged and spent
Sated as you are to unconfined submission....

Natural Affection

Sharon

You are so tenderly wrapped up in love's warm embrace
There's nowhere I'd rather be, you're my happy place
So many nights we've shared heated passion you and I
Fantasies, flowing juices and tangled sheets at night
But it's in these sweet moments of calm quiet and rest
Our soft breathing slow and even, that I love the best
Both unguarded and at peace with no secrets to hide
The sweet smell of sex, cologne and you by my side
Before drifting off to where dreams take me away
I quietly say a prayer, thankful for you every day….

Natural Affection

Ryan

During slumbers shuttered grace I sense your body begin to stir
The ebbs and flow of our bodies writhing, a pleasure that will transfer
Your body responding to my strong arms wrapping around you tight
Being with you, in this moment, feels so good, so right
Ecstasy building as your core begins pulsing, a quickening desire
The heat of our union only increasing in intensity, taking us higher
This resounding joy climaxing in an explosive, powerful flush
We fall into one another, savouring the bodies rush….

Anger

Domestically Violent

Sharon

Time which was once so free and without cost
Passes so quickly, a cruel mockery of life's joy
I wish I knew how to stop these days passing
What has been learned seems wasted on aging moments
The weight of lives lived drawing me near to a future unclear
Caught as I am to the moments between past and present
Burying me under expectation tight embrace
So full of patient grace as I seek compassionate relief
Undeniable is this journeys path, undeniable is its fixed route
Changes hard fought for against corrupted education
A raging transition has been found amongst creative purposes
This strength found with hard lessons
By this will alone will a radiant future be found….

Domestically Violent

Ryan

Words that were once full of love now have a sharp bite
Every encounter challenged by anger and bound to start a fight
His insecure feelings have a way of rising to a rage so hot
At one time this was love but this has now strayed from a caring plot
Manipulative desires have created this prison of their own making
Chained together as they are, she receiving and him taking
Her complicity in belief that change will occur from within
Built upon lies and promises that are abandoned upon a whim
He once said it was this woman that he would cherish and he would adore
It's time to end this vicious cycle, take a stand and say no more….

Confined Silence

Sharon

When I was young, I believed and hoped in all things
I looked at the world around me with idealistic eyes
All too soon my life would change in unexpected ways
Love's tender embrace would be my ultimate downfall
Choices were made with consequences I didn't see
Slowly, trust splintered by my pain and shaken faith
Life should be filled with fantasies and fairy tales
But on a cold fall day I began to notice my gilded cage
Hadn't realized my reality didn't match other's perception
To many, my life looked perfect, they only saw the mask
Where once there was love, I'd become his sick obsession
Often, he said, if he couldn't have me no one else would
Sadly, over time, I believed all his dark and twisted lies
Let this be a cautionary tale, be careful what you wish for
Your monster in the dark might look like Prince charming....

Confined Silence

Ryan

Childhood innocence is a gift to the young
A secret and sacred sanctuary from an uncaring world
Protection granted to children from our pressing reality, a parental desire
It is within this bastion of familiar bonds that form thoughtful foundations
A basis of which will define misunderstood choices and morality's grounding
Pliable as youthful minds are before life hardens thoughts to set ideals
Cynical understanding as ideas blossom to an assertive and expanding ego
This fine line of good intentions misplaced in the angry dissent of righteous opinions
We do our best to refine the noise and articulate unbiased learnings
Simple ideals, kindness, compassion, empathy and sought after connections
Difficult lessons learned during rough history's repeating cycle
To find a voice found amongst the debris of overwhelming ignorant knowledge
Silent no longer and no longer confined by adolescent fear, upon our shoulders they rise….

Depression & Loss

Dreamscape Windows

Sharon

Every night it's always the same haunting nightmare
Always being watched with a deadly, poisonous glare
The dark windows in my mind never letting me escape
If this goes on too much longer I feel that I will break
So many years don't think my soul will ever be at rest
Again I wake up startled and trying to catch my breath
When the sun shines again nothing will have changed
This is my ghostly story I know it must sound strange
One day if you're not careful it could be your life too
If you don't believe me just keep doing what you do….

Dreamscape Windows

Ryan

Windows to dreams seen through the spectre of death
Each fractured dream robbing me of slumber, robbing me of breath
From fields of skulls and winged demons on high
To ashen, pestilent clouds that blacken out the sky
In despair I see all this though the moons cold haze
Rest always elusive I run through the insomniac's maze
Remembered forms lacking substance, they have fallen to consumption
To be free of these memories is a baseless and cruel assumption
Still I persevere with thoughts of solitary dreaming
The knowledge I have gleamed from these horrors makes for fascinating reading
A walking nightmare continues to cloud my thoughtful musing
A blessing or a curse this battle will be of my own choosing....

Continental Drift

Sharon

In the beginning of their relationship love was in full bloom
They had no way of knowing one day it would be doomed
So many things in common so much they would talk about
Then children came along a happy family without a doubt
Careers and commitments and the chaos they can bring
Years passed and they hadn't noticed so many little things
No time for each other and their resentment had grown
Things they might've done different if they'd only known
One day they both realized for them it was much too late
What had started out as a love match had turned to hate....

Continental Drift

Ryan

These two people finding a connection surprisingly yearning
Valuable time spent readily on a friendship worth earning
Each of them finding space in their lives so complicated and distant
Constantly seeking to hold to this moment, this very instant
Clutching tightly to the other's spirit during times of strife
Separation brings about anxiety, biting and sharp as a knife
Ages pass they have found their connection starting to drift
Memories still remain of this friendship, this once in a lifetime gift
Continents cruel division separating these twinned souls
Each knowing the price of distance and willing to pay the tolls
Slowly, bridges are rebuilt over their shared and broken dreams
These two star-crossed souls will meet again and share moonlit themes….

Blue Rain

Sharon

You think you know me, you would be surprised
Looking through me never looking into my eyes
You think you know me I look at you and smile
Looking through me never looking into my eyes
You think you know me there's a side of me I hide
Looking through me never looking into my eyes
You think you know me there's pain deep inside
Looking through me never looking into my eyes
You think you know me my life is full of lies
If you wanna know me look into my eyes….

Blue Rain

Ryan

A prelude to heartbreak, a prelude to pain
Through clouded vision she looks through the rain
Fingers reaching and yearning for a loss so deep
This distant emotion has robbed her of sleep
Eyes bloodshot with tears yet to be shed
She waits on words that will never be said
Still she waits for a love that will be true
Hoping against hope it'll chase away her blues….

Moments in Exile

Sharon

Once upon a time she'd found her handsome prince
He made her happy she felt loved and was convinced
Promises were illusions because of selfish hungry lust
Led astray taking her gift of innocence and her trust
A fairy-tale ended when the princess learned his lies
He had found another princess and tossed her aside
Always wearing a mask her life one of great tragedy
Such a damaged beauty her life now such a travesty
Never trusting anyone though many men have tried
A rare flower sadly never letting anyone else inside….

Moments in Exile

Ryan

Life used to be so colourful, so free from strife
Simple dreams of being a mother, of being a wife
Any hope for a vivid experience is lost in her despair
Why does she still remember the pride before the affair?
This duality of experience has found her spirit diminished
Her illusionist's mask worn, an uneasy proof she is unfinished
She still has her dreams so full of coloured hope
Her story not yet finished and not limited in scope
In sleep and deep slumber she has found a moment's reprieve
This is where she finds her truth and no longer has to deceive
Hidden from all in the most deepest parts of her soul
A pale reflection of who she once was has taken its toll….

Focus

Sharon

It's hard to focus with constant noise and daily distractions
Never sure what to feel so many mixed emotions and reactions
Thousands of thoughts and ideas contemplated and internalized
Always focusing on hopes and dreams that were never realized
Sleep way too often elusive the constant affliction in my brain
Darkness and that familiar feeling of dread always the same
Far too many of my unending days I function as best as I can
From life's twists, turns, tribulations and constant demands
Dwelling is my constant companion never leaving my side
Always been my complacent place where I constantly hide
My wish upon a star is that it won't always be this way
Before my last breath, I'll find peace on that celebrated day….

Focus

Ryan

Fractured, tortured memories have led to this loss of pride
Life passing by, leaving me unable to move aside
Frustrating focus lost, I try to keep the darkness away
This is my battle, one that is fought every day
Days like this are soul crushing, made just for existing
An overwhelming sense of despair, my mind is left twisting
Fading to shadows, I rage against light that has been lost
Pushing away everyone, regardless of the personal cost
The black dog, depression manifest is a path walked alone
A solitary and terrifying journey for sins that I have yet to atone….

In the Shadows

Sharon

I saw her picture remembered who she used to be
The girl everybody loved full of happiness and glee
Married at a tender age to the boy of her dreams
Met when they were kids full of fun and silly schemes
Happy in her youth an exquisite beauty to behold
Her life of promise where together they'd grow old
Was expecting a child on the day she got the call
Her love was taken in such a tragic way as I recall
Her life a Greek tragedy full of sadness and despair
Became a hidden shadow and soon no one cared
The child she wanted who would've saved her life
Was taken that same day and cut her like a knife
There is no happy ending she died on a spring day
For those who mourned her had nothing left to say….

In the Shadows

Ryan

I found you in the shadows, I found you in the night
Eyes heavy, hooded and unable to see the light
It's in this moment that pain has found its mark
This beautiful summer rose, wilting slowly in the dark
How I wish she wouldn't give in to her sorrow
Blind as she is to the hope that is found in tomorrow
Hers is a faith surrendered and given into despair
For all of my compassion, this curse I can't repair
Watching her fade from the woman that I knew her to be
She has gone from this place, leaving only a distant memory….

Karmic Connection

Sharon

They're two lost souls always coming together throughout the ages
Since time began, meant to be together but sadly not for very long
There is an undeniable magical cosmic connection between them
Two lovers in love but circumstances keeping them forever apart
They hear each other's heart beat in the distance calling them home
These tragic star crossed lovers doomed
to repeat their haunted past….

Karmic Connection

Ryan

Our love had made a feast of my soul
All consuming and passionately destructive
Lost identity strung out over reincarnated ages
Each turn of the karmic wheel drawing lovers tight
New life has a way of pulling these distant, fated strands
Regardless of relative distance or baseless timings
Connective spiritual bodies linking tighter together
Ageless death follows closely to separate once more
Another lifetime passes; we fall into entropies' embrace
Solitary heartbeats now scattered amongst strangers
Not quite forgotten, an echo remains of quiet yearning
In this lifetime, in the next lifetime, we will meet again
A guarantee given with the firm conviction of destinies' providence….

Conversation

Sharon

*H*ard to imagine a time when I didn't love you
A love so strong and so much shared passion
*U*ntil you, I never knew what happiness was
*N*ights and days filled with sweet nothings
*T*he mental connection we shared was instant
*E*verything seemed headed for a happily ever after
*D*id I let it slip away or did you, I can't remember?

*L*ost in so many misunderstandings and fights
*O*ur love story has stayed with me for years
*V*ery often I relive those sweet days in my mind
*E*very day that haunted feeling overtakes me….

Haunted Love

Ryan

Communication found so easily at relationship's beginning
Ordinary discussion pushed aside, it's depth that they are seeking
Noticed, focussed attention upon a connection immediately deep
Vigorous as this introduction is and surprisingly essential
Easing into an easy ebb and flow of commitment's new bliss
Relishing this known heart for it rhythm beats easily as one
Shared and stated goals readily blur into a singular vision
Attached monogamy a given during this comfortable transition
Tension sometimes showing where once there was effortless joy
Intimacy strained when life's pressures corrode weakening foundations
Only the strong shall survive these times as they are changing
Never regretting what was for the pain is a reminder it was real….

Earthly Future

Planetary Dreaming

Sharon

When I was little, playing outside with my friends
Life was a constant adventure I never saw an end

I remember water under my bare feet in the creek
Breathing in fresh air, playing baseball on the street

Walks in the woods picking wildflowers in the fields
Running free such a beautiful world it was all real

Now that I'm older and have children of my own
The water poisoned from sources still unknown

The air from polluted factories with its thick smoke
We can't catch our breath as we wheeze and choke

The blue skies of old are now overcast and grey
My hope for the future sadly dwindles every day

All I have now are memories of what used to be
Knowing past beauty kids of today will never see....

Planetary Dreaming

Ryan

Wistful dreaming of this planet far above
A verdant planet that I have come to love
Pristine landscapes I can proudly voice
No place in this sanctuary from destructive choice
Elusive as sleep is I can still find this place
A haven filled with longing and distant pure grace
Still I persist in finding peace in solitary reflection
Nightmares forgotten briefly while admiring perfection
How I wish I could share this home with those that I cherish
Unfortunately this not to be as waking dreams perish....

Worldly Tears

Sharon

Children played carefree with their friends outside
Depravity now the way in a world filled with lies
Jobs were plentiful, loyalty rewarded, people cared
Now a steady job hard to find and goods ones rare
Families went to church worshipped and prayed
Today faith is shaken and torn apart every day
Kids from broken homes not sure which way to turn
So much murder and hate it's all they have learned
Unless people finally wake up and see what's ahead
The world will get worse filled with fear and dread….

Worldly Tears

Ryan

Where in heavens name did we go so wrong?
A forgotten memory of unity amongst the throng
When was the time that we lost our imperfect grace?
We seem to forget we are all part of the same race
Grasping for possessions, this isn't what we need
Nothing seems to slow our relentless, unmitigated greed
The huddled masses breathing air that's thick and cloying
Our world, our home we are slowly destroying
A global problem why isn't this something we can sense
Thinking of the future we leave for others makes us tense
Those selfish people ignoring this proof, a narcissistic denial
It's hoped we'll see the light for our own survival….

About the Authors

Sharon Johnson

Sharon Johnson, has been writing since she was 6 years old. She had one dream, to become a published author. Year after year the book never came. Until the summer of 2013 when a two to three page idea max kept growing and before long, it became clear, her characters had much more to say and their story was far from over. That's how 'The Chat Room' was born. Eighteen months and a lifetime later, her dream finally became a reality in August 2015.

She has seven previously published books:

1. The Chat Room
2. His Second Chance Love
3. Poetry of the Heart
4. The Eclectic Poet & Friends
5. Eclectic Poet My Voice
6. Letters Away A Love Story (Co-authored with Elias Raven)
7. Letters Away A Love Story Prequel (Co-authored with Elias Raven)

To find out more about Sharon, you can follow her on her author Facebook page;

https://www.facebook.com/Sharon-Johnson-Author-Poet-1675818972688542/

Twitter:
https://twitter.com/srjohns53

Amazon

https://www.amazon.com/SharonJohnson/e/B018Q61H4C/ref=dp_byline_cont_ebooks_1

Barnes & Noble

http://www.barnesandnoble.com/w/letters-away-elias-raven/1125496180?ean=9781508050100

Ryan Baird

Ryan Baird is a poet and wordsmith, using a combination of different poetic styles and themes. As he has honed his writing skills he has branched out into different poetic styles which include, free verse, haiku, rhyming, acrostic and double acrostic poems covering a broad range of emotional musings. When he's not working as a Drill and Blast Trainer/Assessor on a faraway mine site in Australia, he can be found in his man cave at home seeking the cathartic release that only writing will give.

He's also the author of:

Private Ryan Volume 1

To find out more about Ryan, you can follow him on his author Facebook page;

https://www.facebook.com/PrivateRyan2372/?fref=ts

Twitter:

https://twitter.com/Pte_Ryan

Instagram:

https://www.instagram.com/pte_ryan/

Amazon:

http://amzn.to/2kbRqNw